Duct Tape

Your *heart* Out!

LEISURE ARTS, INC.
Maumelle, Arkansas

EDITORIAL STAFF
Vice President of Editorial: Susan White Sullivan
Publications Director: Leah Lampirez
Creative Art Director: Katherine Laughlin
Special Projects Director: Susan Frantz Wiles
Special Projects Designer: Patti Wallenfang
Design Assistant: Kelly Reider
Technical Editor: Jean W. Lewis
Contributing Editor: Mary Sullivan Hutcheson
Art Category Manager: Lora Puls
Graphic Artist: Becca Snider Tally
Prepress Technician: Stephanie Johnson
Contributing Photo Stylist: Lori Wenger
Contributing Photographers: Mark Mathews and
    Ken West
Director of E-Commerce and Prepress Services:
    Mark Hawkins
Manager of E-Commerce: Robert Young

BUSINESS STAFF
President and Chief Executive Officer: Rick Barton
Senior Vice President of Operations: Jim Dittrich
Vice President of Finance: Fred F. Pruss
Vice President of Sales-Retail Books: Martha Adams
Vice President of Mass Market: Bob Bewighouse
Vice President of Technology and Planning:
    Laticia Mull Dittrich
Information Technology Director: Brian Roden
Controller: Tiffany P. Childers
Retail Customer Service Manager: Stan Raynor

ISBN-13: 978-1-4647-1501-3

Contents

DUCKS ON A POND (shown right)
Strips of Ducklings™ transform a basic
yellow duck family into a cute & colorful
brood. Just cover the bodies with short
tape strips & add narrow neck rings in
contrasting colors. Float your duck family
on a pond cut from a double-sided duct
tape sheet (page 46). The bowl on Mama
Duck's back is the perfect place to keep
your Ducklings™ handy & dry.

With today's colorful duct tape & the fun projects in this book, you can craft to your heart's content! Dress up school stuff & rain gear, make hip headphones & a purse or wallet, give new life to old shoes, bend covered co-ax cable into wall art words & create unique jewelry to share with friends. These ideas are irresistible! Step-by-step photos & clear instructions make it all super easy.

DUCK® vs. duct

For the record...DUCK® is the brand of tape that is featured in this book, and is a registered trademark of ShurTech Brands, LLC, Avon, OH.

Duct tape is the generic product description for the type of tape used in this book.

Only duct tape distributed by ShurTech Brands, LLC has the right to be called "DUCK TAPE®". When shopping for your duct tape, be sure to look for the Trust E. Duck logo (shown above) to ensure you are getting the original DUCK® brand quality!

Locker Décor

MIRROR

Cover the frame of a locker-size mirror with tape strips. To make the fans that go around the frame, fold a 2$^1/_2$" long tape piece onto itself.

leave some sticky stuff showing

Gather the tape & stick on the mirror back. Keep adding fans until the mirror is full.

A few tape strips hold everything in place. Add more magnet strips to the back.

FLOWER MAGNET

For each petal, fold a 5" long tape piece onto itself. Freehand cut the petals.

leave some sticky stuff showing

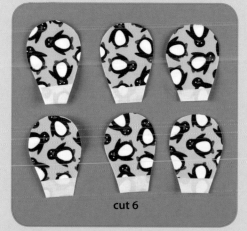

cut 6

Tape the petals together.

Add a circle of tape & a pic to the center. Glue a magnet on the back.

BOW MAGNET

Fold a 2$^1/_2$" tape piece onto itself. Fold another one.

leave some sticky stuff showing

Gather the tape & stick them together, end to end.

Wrap the center with a short $^1/_4$" strap (page 46) & glue a magnet on the back.

Cool Stuff

For the petals, fold a 2" tape strip onto itself. Cut the strip in half & round off the corners. Make 8 petals.

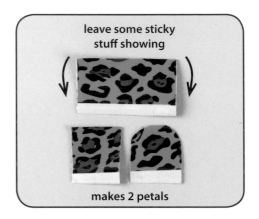

leave some sticky stuff showing

makes 2 petals

Tape the petals around the flower center.

HEADPHONES

Start by stickin' some tape strips on the headband part of the headphones. Then add some flowers to the ear pieces.

For the flower center, wad up a bit of paper & stick it to the ear piece with tape.

Wrap a narrow tape strip over the inner petal edges to seal it all together.

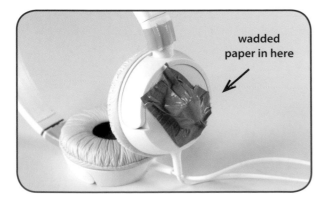

wadded paper in here

BACKPACK

Dress up the flaps on a BORING backpack with leftover bits of tape. Then, you'll be real cool in school.

Shoes & Boots

DESSED-UP FLATS

Give new life to well-loved shoes with a duct tape facelift. Add just a strip or two across the toes or completely cover your shoes with an overall patterned tape. Have fun with this one!

And of course the box can be just as cute—cover the lid with tape & border it with a narrow strip (a Duckling™ works great for this).

BOOTS

Using 3"-6" tape pieces & overlapping any which way, cover the boot top. Trim the tape ends even with the top edge.

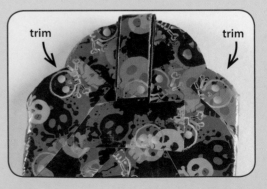

Clean up the edges (page 48) between the top & bottom.

SASSY SLIP-ONS

Starting at the center back with a horizontal strip & working toward the front, cover the back & sides with tape (page 46); add a contrasting strip to the back.

For the front, cover the top with tape strips. Clean up the edges (page 48) between the top & sole.

Trim the tape to expose the elastic. Add contrasting narrow trim strips to the inside & outside of the shoe.

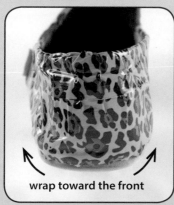

wrap toward the front

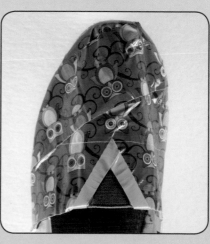

Accessories

BRAIDED BRACELET

Make three ¼" straps about 12" long (page 46) & tape together.

Braid the straps. Tape the braid together at the desired bracelet length.

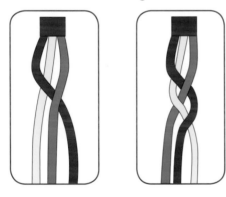

Cut eight 12" lengths of embroidery floss or craft cord (ribbon would work too!). Tape 4 pieces to each bracelet end.

RING

Make three ⅛" straps about 6" long (page 46) & braid them (see the photos & diagrams on the left). Tape the braid into a ring.

STRETCHY BRACELET

Take an elastic ponytail holder & turn it into a super cool bracelet (left). Just add rings of tape (Ducklings™ are perfect for this!) made from $1/4$" straps (page 46). There are so many colorful elastics, you can make several for all your friends!

HEADBAND

Make three $1/4$" straps about 15" long (page 46) & braid them (see the photos & diagrams on the left). Tape the braid ends to a headband.

Add a snappy bow if you're in the mood (see page 5 for instructions). For a different look, just stick a strip of tape to a headband & add a bow.

School Stuff

MINI NOTEBOOK

Cover the notebook cover with tape strips. A colorful bow (see the instructions on page 5) can jazz up the cover too!

Make a ¹/₂" strap (page 46) that is about 6" long. Slide it through the notebook rings & tape together.

FOLDER

Customize your folders with tape strips in varying widths (Ducklings™ are good for this!). Use 3 tapes, 6 tapes, 8 tapes, as many as you wish!

HANGING ORGANIZER

Cover 3 zipper-style plastic sandwich bags with tape.

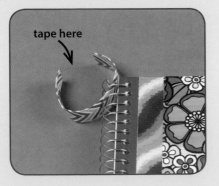

tape here

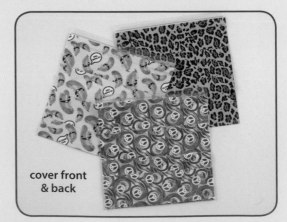

cover front & back

Overlap the bags about 2" & tape together with ³/₄" strips (or use a Duckling™).

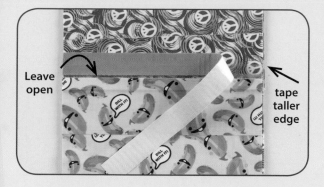

Make two ³/₄" x 3" straps (page 46); tape to the organizer back. Tape around the top edge. Glue strong magnetic strips to the back.

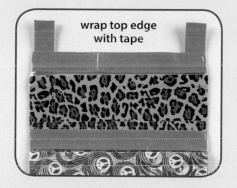

wrap top edge with tape

For the flower, make a 15" double-sided strip (page 47) & punch small holes along one edge. Weave yarn or string through the punched holes; pull the yarn ends to gather.

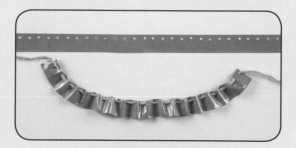

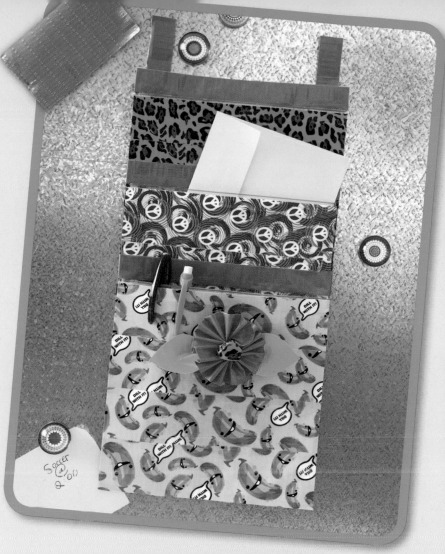

For the flower center, push a tape wad through the flower center & tape in place on wrong side.

make a tape wad

For the leaves, make a double-sided green strip & freehand cut 2 leaves.

Tape the leaves & flower to the organizer.

knot on back

Bedroom Décor

NIGHTSTAND

Create a one-of-a-kind nightstand for your room. Choose a variety of tapes, mostly prints, but be sure to include a least 1 solid. Get a Duckling™ for the drawer knob.

Start by placing a tape strip in the middle of the nightstand top.

Next, go around & around that piece with some other tapes until the whole top is covered.

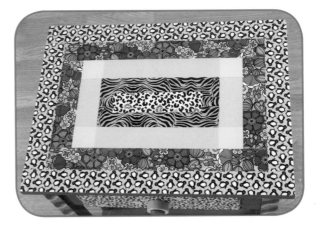

Then cover the legs with another print tape.

For the drawer, remove the knob. Cover the front with tape. Slide a Duckling™ onto the knob shaft & re-attach the knob.

CLOCK

Dress out your clock with chunks of tape. A $1/4$" strap (page 46) tied into a bow around the top gives the clock a funky flair.

LAMP SHADE

Ducklings™ work great for this project.

For each flower, make three ³/₄" x 8" double-sided strips (page 47).

Make five ³/₈" x 6" double-sided strips or just fold Duckling™ strips in half.

Punch a hole in the center & near each end of each strip.

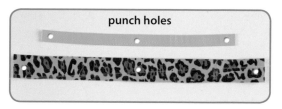

punch holes

Fold the ends to the center & stack the wide then narrow strips on a brad.

brad

Glue a button to the flower center; glue each flower to the shade. Trim the shade with some tape strips

Paper Clip Jewelry

MIX IT UP
Necklace
Hook 2 paper clips together.

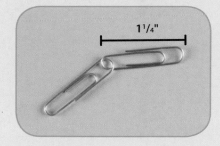

Wrap 1 clip with a ³/₄" x 1" tape piece.

Add another clip & wrap.

Continue adding & wrapping clips until your necklace is the right length (we used 25 clips for a 30" necklace).

Hook the last clip to the first & wrap.

Double Bracelet
For the plain bracelet, wrap & join 7 clips together to make an 8³/₄" bracelet (see necklace left). Add or delete clips to make your bracelet the right size. Tie the ends together with elastic cord.

For the beaded bracelet, slip 2 silver beads on a paper clip. Keeping 1 bead at each end of the clip, wrap & join 7 clips (add or delete clips to make your bracelet the right size). Tie the ends together with elastic cord.

Tie the 2 bracelets together with a multi-ribbon bow.

Earrings
For each earring, slip beads on 2 paper clips. Wrap clips with a ³/₄" x 1" tape piece. Use a jump ring (page 47) to attach the clips to an earring wire.

add beads before wrapping

LEOPARD
Use leopard tape & follow Mix It Up (left) to make a necklace, a plain bracelet with a bow & earrings with three clips.

RAINBOW
Using rainbow tape & bright-colored pony beads, follow Mix It Up (left) to make a beaded necklace, bracelet with a bow & earrings with two clips (add beads before wrapping).

add beads before wrapping

Messenger Bag

Finished Size:
11"w x 9"h with a 5" flap

Make an 11" x 23" single-sided sheet (page 46) for the bag lining. For the bag outside, place six 23" long tape strips on a cutting mat side by side. Cover the seams with a half width of tape (or just use a Duckling™).

Make a double-sided sheet (page 46) with the lining & bag outside. Trim to 22" long. Cover 1 short edge (page 46). Fold the sheet & cover the long edges.

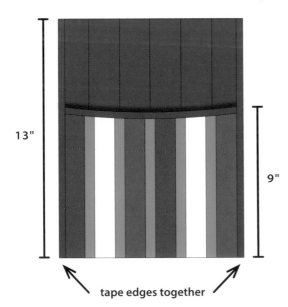

13"

9"

tape edges together

Make a 1" x 38" strap (page 46) & tape to the bag back.

tape down

Cut a 3" tape strip & fold into a triangle. Make 5 triangles.

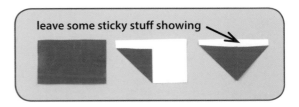

leave some sticky stuff showing

Stick the triangles on the flap.

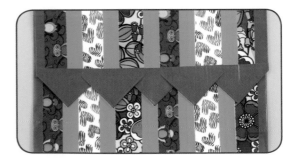

Decorate the flap with tape strips.

Punch 2 holes in the flap at the center. Make a $1/4$" x 9" strap & tie it through the punched holes.

punch holes

Frog Tablet Case

TABLET CASE

Cover the front of a 7" x 9" padded mailing envelope with blue tape & the back with green tape.

Stick a strip of blue tape around the inside top edge of the envelope.

Make a single-sided green sheet (page 46). Use the pattern (page 45) to cut a frog.

Stick the frog to the envelope front.

Use the patterns to cut 2 white eyes, 2 black pupils & a pink tongue from tape.

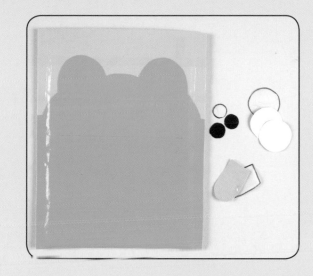

Stick the shapes to the envelope front. Draw a mouth with a marker. Cut a small half-circle finger hole in the center of the front top edge.

Party Time

PARTY BANNER

Make 3 pink, 3 green & 4 yellow 6" x 6"double-sided sheets (page 46). Cut a triangle from each sheet.

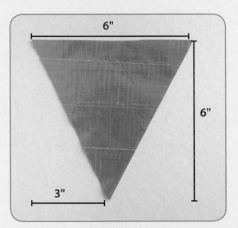

Cover the edges (page 46) with $3/4$" tape strips.

Add a stick-on letter to each triangle.

Punch holes in the top corners. Join the "P A R T Y" & the "T I M E" triangles with $1/4$" x $2^1/2$" straps (page 46) threaded through the holes & taped together.

Use $1/2$" x 6" straps to make & attach "chains" to the banner ends.

tape 1st chain together

slide new chains thru joined chains & tape together

MASON JAR GLASSES

Make double-sided strips (page 47) in several colors. Cut a triangle for each letter of a name.

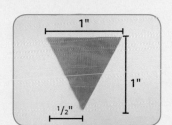

MUSTACHE DRINKING STRAWS

Make a black double-sided sheet (page 46). Use the pattern on page 43 to cut mustaches from the sheet.

Stick the mustaches to drinking straws with strips of black tape.

Attach the triangles to a long yarn piece with narrow tape strips. Spell out the name with rub-on letters.

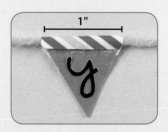

Wrap the jar lids with tape strips (Ducklings™ work great for this) & tie the banners on the jars.

23

Party Favors

DUCKLING™ "CANDY"

For a cute "just because" gift, wrap a Duckling™ tape roll in a piece of cellophane (get this in the party supply section). Tie the ends with curling ribbon.

CANDY TUBE

Find a cardboard tube about 6" long (paper towel roll, gift wrap roll, bathroom tissue roll) & cover it with tape.

Place some candy in a sandwich baggie & seal shut. Slide the baggie into the covered tube.

Wrap the candy tube in a 12" x 12" piece of cellophane (get this in the party supply section). Tie the ends with curling ribbon.

Flower Bouquet

Ducklings™ work great for this project.

FLOWER BOUQUET

Flower

For each flower, make three ³/₄" x 8" double-sided strips (page 47).

Make five ³/₈" x 6" double-sided strips or just fold a Duckling™ strip in half.

Layering the narrow then wide strips on the brad, follow flower instructions on page 15.

brad

For each stem, cover a drinking straw with tape.

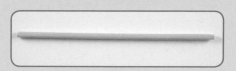

For each leaf, make a ³/₄" x 10" double-sided tape strip; trim 1 end to a point (for stiffer leaves you can sandwich a length of thin wire between the tape strips).

Tape 1 or 2 leaves to each stem.

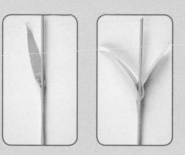

Tape a flower to each stem.

Vase

Wrap a mason jar lid with a ³/₄" tape strip.

Refer to page 5 to make the bow. Tape the bow to the jar.

Tag

Make a 2" x 3¹/₂" double-sided strip.

Add narrow tape strips; trim 1 end.

punch hole here

Arrange the flowers in the vase then fill the vase with candies. Tie the tag on with cord.

Duct tape not recommended for food contact.

Purses

Add tape accents to the purse. We cut a curved design in the tape ends.

Personalize the purse with an alphabet sticker.

LATTICE FLAP PURSE

The flap on our purse is 7" x 7" & we used about 5 yards total of ¼" wide straps (page 46) for the lattice and tassel. Your purse may be a different size, but you'll still need lots of strap pieces!

For the flap, start just off-center & measure from the back edge of the flap to the front edge; add 1½". Make a ¼" strap this long. Using small pieces of tape to hold the ends in place, tape this strap to the flap diagonally.

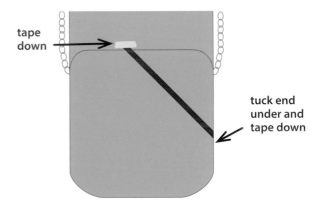

tape down

tuck end under and tape down

PINK PURSE

Transform a cute, but a bit plain, see-through purse with tape. If the purse has a shoulder strap, cover 1 side of the strap with tape. For shorter handles, make tape "handle grips".

Move over about 1" on either side of the 1st strap, measure and make two ¼" straps these measurements; tape in place. Continue adding straps until the flap is covered with diagonal straps.

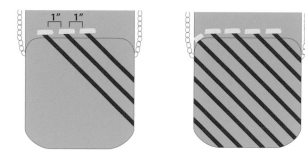

Starting just off-center with a ¼" strap, weave the strap over and under each right diagonal strap; tape in place on wrong side of flap.

Continue adding ¼" straps until the flap is covered. Add tape to cover the strap ends.

Make a single-sided sheet (page 46) on non-stick foil. Draw around the flap and cut out. Remove the sheet & stick to the wrong side of the flap.

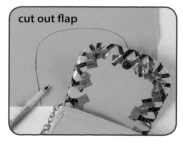

cut out flap

cut a hole for magnet

For the tassel, make eight 6" straps. Fold the straps over a cord length & wrap with a ¾" contrasting tape strip. Knot the cord just above the folded straps.

knot cord

wrap with tape

cut fringe

Tie the tassel to the purse with the cord.

Rain Gear

RAIN GEAR

Go splishing & splashing in a tape-decorated raincoat & rain boots.

For the boots, add some tape strips around the boot tops. Use the patterns (page 44) to cut some raindrops. Stick the raindrops on the boots.

For the raincoat, trim the collar, front edges, bottom edge, sleeve edges, & pocket flaps with tape strips.

Make tape appliqués (page 47) with the patterns on page 44. Be sure to reverse the patterns for one duckie.

Stick the appliqués on the pockets. Glue wiggle eyes to the duckies.

Sit-Upon Game Day Cushion

CUSHION

Make two 14" x 14" single-sided sheets (page 46). Decorate 1 sheet with assorted tape widths & a tape monogram.

For the padding, use 13" x 13" squares of batting, thin foam, or layered newspaper to make the padding the thickness you desire. Sandwich the padding between the sheets. Staple around the cushion edges.

padding

sticky side down

sticky side up

Cover the edges (page 46) with 1" tape strips.

Make three ³/₄" x 42" straps (page 46). Tape the ends together & braid; tape the remaining ends together.

Securely tape the strap to the cushion back with 3 tape strips.

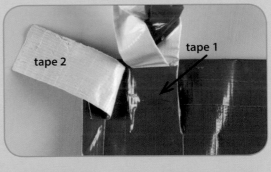

tape 2

tape 1

tape 3

Lunchtime

LUNCH SACK
Carefully open a paper lunch sack.

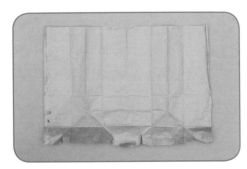

Cover each side with tape strips. We used clear tape on the inside.

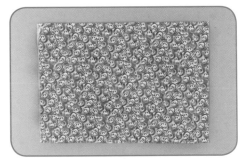

Refold the bag & tape the back & bottom closed. Cover the top edge (page 46).

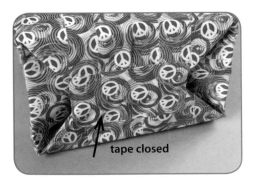

tape closed

Add a strip down the front & up the back, folding 2" of tape onto itself to make the closure. Stick a hook & loop fastener on the closure & the sack front.

REUSABLE SANDWICH BAG
Cover the front of a heavy-duty zipper-top food bag.

quart-size freezer storage bag

Date:

Cover the tape edges with narrow strips of tape in a contrasting color.

You can also just put one strip on the bag; then cut out shapes from the tape & stick them on. Cover the edges (page 46) & add a narrow strip at the top.

HAND SANITIZER CARRYALL
Make a $1/2$" strap (page 46) that is about 12" longer than the bottle's height. Tape the strap ends together.

bottle height + 12"

$1

Fresh Vanilla hand sanitizer

Center the bottle on the strap &
wrap with tape.

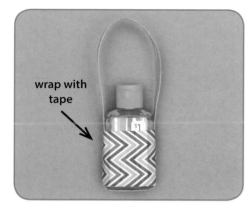

wrap with
tape

DRESSED UP
HAND SANITIZER

Cut some tape into the shape
of the label & stick it over the
label. Add a narrow strip around
the neck & a blingy topper for a
personalized germ chaser.

Duct tape not
recommended for
food contact.

Jackets

JACKETS

Show your style with these tape-trimmed faux leather jackets. Start by covering the collar edges with tape.

Then add strips to the lower edge, center front, shoulder seams, sleeves, wherever you like.

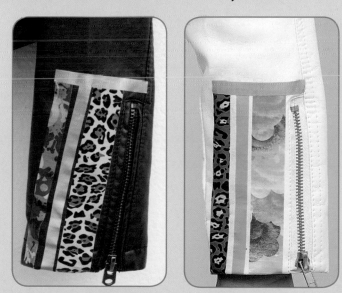

We added a layered appliqué (page 47) to the white jacket using the heart pattern on page 43. Try using decorative-edge scissors to cut one of the hearts. Make a bow (page 5) & glue it to the heart.

Trim the jacket with charms & pendants. Just attach them with tape-covered paper clips (page 17). Glue on fake jewels for some added sparkle.

Wallets

BASIC WALLET

Make a double-sided sheet (page 46) with 2 different tapes.

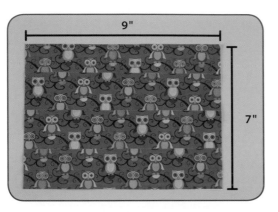

Fold the sheet; tape the sides together.

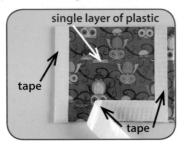

tape here & here

Add a clear plastic badge holder to the inside.

single layer of plastic

tape

tape

Make a 16" double-sided strip (page 47). Cover the top edge (page 46) & cut 4 pockets.

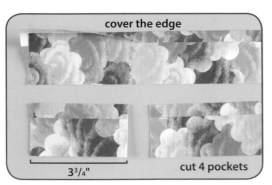

cover the edge

3³/₄"

cut 4 pockets

Stack the pockets & tape to the wallet. Fold the wallet in half.

tape

UNION JACK WALLET

Make a Basic Wallet (left) with blue & white tapes.

Cut four ³/₄" x 6" white strips. Cut two ³/₄" x 6" red strips & four ¹/₄" x 3" red strips.

Make a "+" & then an "x" with the wide white strips; trim. Make an offset "x" with the narrow red strips; trim.

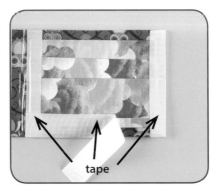

trim the edges

Make a "+" with the wide red strips; trim.

Cover the Union Jack sides with blue tape strips.

DILL WITH IT WALLET

Make a Basic Wallet (left) with dill pickle, white & silver tapes.

Use the patterns on page 43, to cut sunglasses, a large circle, & a large speech bubble from black tape. Cut a small circle, & a small speech bubble from white tape. Stick the shapes to the wallet front.

Add a message to the speech bubble.

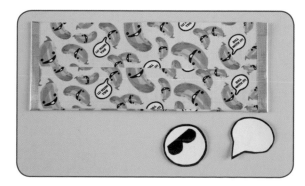

Boxes

NEON SCHOOL BOXES

Cover the top of a metal box with assorted-size tape strips (we used an 8" x 4" x 2$^1/_2$" school box).

Use layered tape strips & a stick-on initial to personalize the box.

GIFT BOXES

Make a double-sided sheet (page 46). Use the patterns (right) to cut a lid & bottom from the sheet.

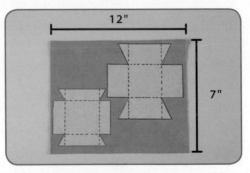

For the lid, fold & crease on the dashed lines. Tuck the side points inside the straight sides & secure with tape.

fold in & tape

Clipping at inside corners as needed, cover the edges (page 46) with a $^3/_4$" strip. Ducklings™ work well for this. Cover the sides with a contrasting $^3/_4$" strip.

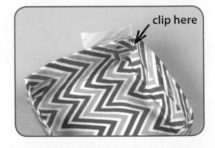

clip here

For the bottom, fold & tape the inside corners like the lid. Secure each outside corner with a $^3/_4$" strip. Cover the edges with a $^3/_4$" strip.

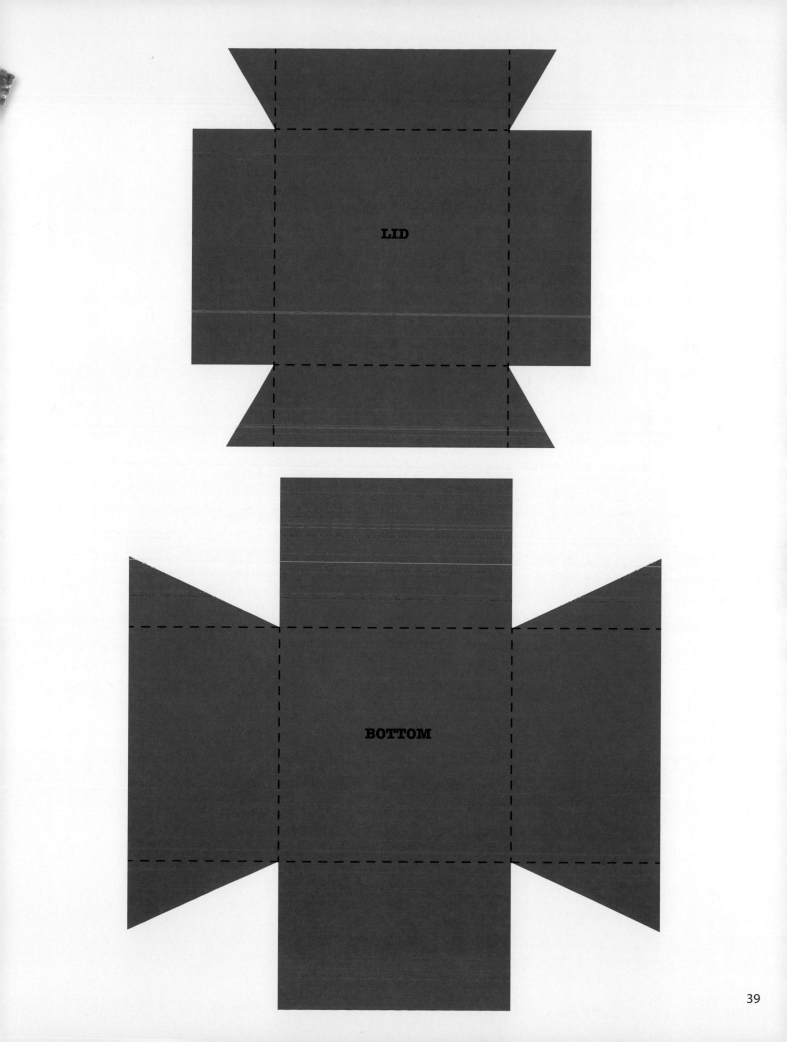

BRACELETS

SPIKE BRACELET

Make a $^3/_4$" x wrist-size strap.

Fold $1^1/_2$" tape strips into triangles.

$1^1/_2$"

Stick a triangle to the strap & wrap tape to the back.

wrap to the back

Overlapping by $^1/_2$", add triangles to cover the strap.

Add a $^3/_4$" strip to the inside of the bracelet & a hook & loop fastener piece to each end.

DUCT TAPE BEADS BRACELETS

To make the "beads", cut a plastic drinking straw into 1/2" pieces. Roll a 1/2" x 8" tape strip around each straw piece.

For the yellow & pink satin cord bracelet, fold a 72" length of each color in half. Insert the folds into a side-release plastic buckle piece & pull the ends through the loop.

tighten

Tape the buckle down. With yellow, tie a square knot (page 47) around the pink cords. Reverse colors & tie a pink knot around the yellow cords; repeat.

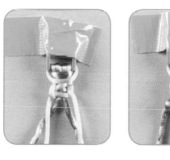

Slide a bead up the 2 yellow cords & tie a square knot with the pink cords.

Tying a square knot between each bead, add 2 more beads. Reversing colors after each knot, tie 4 more square knots.

Slip the cord ends through the remaining buckle piece, tuck the ends under the last knot & trim; glue to secure.

You can also make a cool bracelet for a guy. Just follow same the instructions, but use black & tan paracord!

Duck®-script Wall Art

Frame a rectangle (we used corrugated plastic, but you could use wood, stiff poster board, or foam core) with strips of tape.

Wrap tape lengths around co-ax cable, stiff rope, plastic tubing or any other round material that bends easily (we used co-ax cable).

Form an "L" & "ove" with the cable.

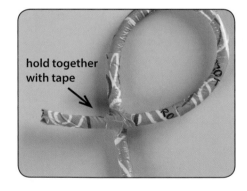

hold together with tape

Glue the word to the rectangle.

Use the pattern on page 43 to cut a heart from a single-sided sheet (page 46). Stick the heart on the rectangle.

Patterns

DUCK®-SCRIPT
WALL ART

DILL WITH IT
WALLET

MUSTACHE
DRINKNG
STRAWS

JACKETS

RAIN GEAR

FROG TABLET CASE

Basics

MAKING A SINGLE-SIDED SHEET

Stick the tape end to a cutting mat & roll out. Cut the strip from the roll. Cut the strips a bit longer than the size you need.

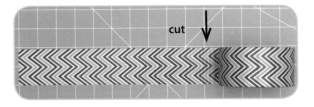

Stick a second strip to the mat, overlapping the first. Keep adding strips until you have the right size sheet.

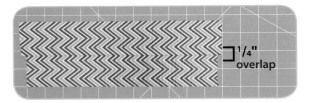

MAKING A DOUBLE-SIDED SHEET

Make 2 Single-Sided Sheets, cutting the strips a bit longer than you need. Stick the sheets to each other; trim to the right size.

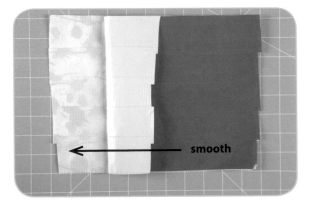

COVERING AN EDGE

Trim a piece of tape to the desired width. The projects use $1/4$", $3/4$", & 1". Place the edge about halfway over the tape strip; fold the strip down.

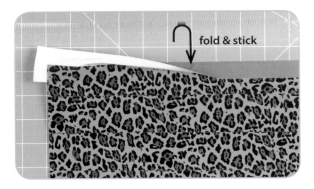

MAKING A STRAP

Cut a tape strip the indicated length. Trim the width (see below). Place the tape, sticky side up, on the cutting mat. Fold one long edge about $1/3$ of the way toward the middle.

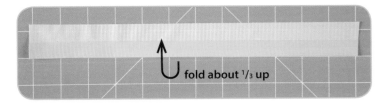

Fold down the other long edge & smooth.

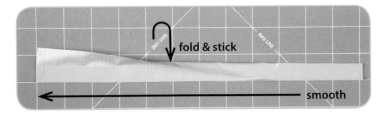

More Strap Info

The strips are 3x the width of the finished strap.

$3/8$" strip = $1/4$" wide strap
$3/4$" strip = $1/4$" wide strap
$1^1/2$" strip = $1/2$" wide strap
$2^1/4$" pieced strip = $3/4$" wide strap
3" pieced strip = 1" wide strap

MAKING A DOUBLE-SIDED STRIP
Cut 2 strips of tape & stick to each other.

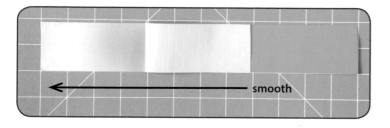

smooth

MAKING TAPE APPLIQUÉS
Trace the patterns onto paper & cut out. Make a pattern for each piece of the appliqué.

trace patterns

Make a Single-Sided Sheet (on non-stick foil) to fit the pattern. Draw around the pattern on the sheet; cut out the appliqué & peel away the foil.

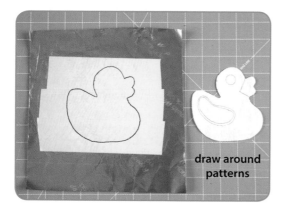

draw around patterns

Stack the smaller appliqué pieces on the larger ones on a cutting mat. Then stick the whole thing on your project.

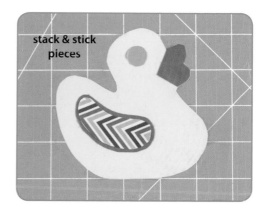

stack & stick pieces

OPENING & CLOSING A JUMP RING
To open, use 2 pairs of pliers to push 1 side of jump ring away while pulling the other side toward you.

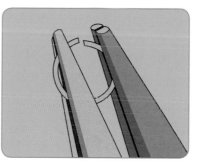

To close, push & pull ring in opposite directions.

SQUARE KNOT

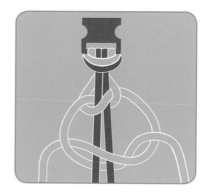

47

CLEANING UP THE EDGES

Use your fingernail, an ink pen, or the tip of a blunt knife or nail file to crease the tape between the sole & shoe or to follow a shape (like the curve of a boot top). Lift the tape & trim on the crease line; stick tape back down.

 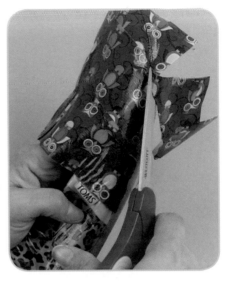

Duct Tape Tips

Working with duct tape is quick & easy! Here are a few tips we picked up while building these projects, but there are endless techniques. Get creative & have fun!

- Scissors work for cutting small pieces of tape & clipping curves. Non-stick scissors are great for cutting duct tape.

- It's super quick to use a craft knife & metal ruler when cutting strips & sheets. Craft knives are sharp & safety is important.

- A self-healing cutting mat protects the table & has lots of guidelines for measuring & aligning the tape strips. To remove the tape from the mat, use the tip of the knife blade to pick up a corner of the tape.

- Once you've stuck 2 pieces of tape together, smooth your finger or hand over the overlapped areas to make sure they really stick.